From a Garden...
to a Forest

Two Plays for the Environment

by
Darren Vallier

Jasper Publishing

1 Broad St Hemel Hempstead Herts HP2 5BW
Tel; 01442 63461 Fax; 01442 217102

Jasper Publishing

1 Broad Street Hemel Hempstead
Herts HP2 5BW
Tel; 01442 63461 Fax; 01442 217102

ISBN 1 874009 52 X

FROM A GARDEN...

TO A FOREST

(Two Plays for the Environment)

THE IVORY FOREST

and

THE GARDEN PLOT

MUSIC

**Suitable music and songs for these two plays
can be found in**

The Darren Vallier Song Book

Published by Jasper Publishing

In many cases the songs have been specially written to suit.

Alternatively, the Musical Director is free to prepare, in
collaboration with the students, music that reflects their own
interpretation of the spirit of the plays

THE IVORY FOREST

A Play by Darren Vallier

Burning, farming, logging, mining and ranching has destroyed over half the Amazon Forest. Experts predict that the entire Forest will be destroyed within the next hundred years. The Amazon is dying. We must all become keepers of the Forest... The Ivory Forest!

This is a Musical Play based on the feelings of the Animals found in the Amazon Forest when they are faced with the evil Ranchers' plans to burn the Forest down no matter what the consequences! A humorous, yet poignant story with a clear environmental message. Suggestions have been made throughout the script regarding the types of songs that could be included to either reinforce certain messages or enhance certain scenes

This play was first performed at Patcham Junior School in July 1994

CHARACTERS

Characters are based on the types of Animals and Creatures that might be found in such an environment. Any of these Animal parts can be changed or adapted to suit your particular production

Main Character Parts are as follows

> A Do Do
> Noah Junior
> The Narrators - 6 main parts
> The Ranchers - 7 main parts
> The Vultures - 4 main parts

Other Characters with speaking parts include

> Leopards
> Bees
> Parrots
> Elephants
> Butterflies
> Monkeys
> Baboons
> Beetles
> Toad
> Panda

Any number of children could represent these Animals and therefore be part of the chorus to help with the singing or music

THE IVORY FOREST

The Scene is set in a colourful Amazon Forest/Jungle setting

Typical forest sounds can be heard

The play opens as Forest Animals hold still life positions around the acting area. Levels should be used to create the effect of power, size, domination. Suddenly the silence is broken with whispers from the different sets of Animals

Leopards and **Monkeys**   Forest!
Elephants   Forest!
Parrots   Tangled!
Baboons   Species!
Bees   Shelter!
Butterflies   Emerald!
Leopards and **Monkeys**   Forest!
Bats   Steamy!
Ranchers   Water!
Vultures   Precious!
Main Characters   Keeper!
All   Ivory Forest!

All Animals put their heads down and the Narrators who are placed around the acting area begin to say their piece as slow piano music is played underneath

Music No 1

A slow instrumental piano melody. Perhaps the melody of the final chorus song could be used

Narrator 1   This year, an area the size of Belgium will be cut down and destroyed beyond all hope of recovery.
Narrator 2   Beautiful trees, 200 feet tall, with tangled branches will be burnt to the ground.
Narrator 3   We will lose 100 species of Animals and insects every day.
Narrator 4   There will soon be no air... no medicines!
Narrator 5   The Forest is being stolen from us!
Narrator 6   The Forest is dying!

Music No 2

Uptempo Chorus number as the animals wake up

The Narrators sit back down as the Animals come to life and continue with their daily routines and habits. A Do Do enters and begins to address the different groups of Animals. The Animals ignore her, and each time she speaks, they simply turn away from her. The Do Do sounds upset

Do Do Butterflies, Butterflies, I've just heard something really important. Leopards, we are going to need your hel...p...
Elephants! You'll listen to me when I tell you that the Ranchers are going to...
Baboons, we must do something otherwise the Forest will...
Oh won't anyone listen to what I have to say?

The scene changes and we see a group of rather nasty looking Ranchers playing cards and cheating rather badly. They suddenly realise that they are being watched and so quickly throw the cards over their shoulder and rise into a tough 'macho' stance. The Ranchers talk in gruff voices. A group of Vultures are perched listening to what is being said. They chuckle quietly to themselves

Big Mac 'Cos we are... *(motif)*

All the Ranchers join in the Motif together. They spit on each hand, wipe it down the shirt and then jump to the left whilst pointing with their right hand

All The Ranchers!
Mac Big Mac.
Ken Ken Tucky.
Pete Pete Zerut.
Maurice Maurice, the Little Chef.
Sam Uncle Sam.
Wimpy *(in a pathetic voice)* Wimpy!
King Burger King.
All You got it.
Mac We're gonna burn down them trees.
All Yeah!
King It's gonna be a wipe out.
All Yeah!
Pete We're gonna make Burgers.
Sam As far as the eye can see.
Maurice Buns!

Ken Mayonnaise!
Mac Mustard!
Pete Big Ones!
King Juicy Ones!
Wimpy But we must remember that Vegetarians are important too!

They all look at him and pause

All Daaaaa!
Sam Small furry things in a sandwich!
Maurice Feathered Meat!
Mac Loads of Meat!
Ken That's all Animals are good for...
Pete Eating and Burning!
Maurice Okay Smartie Pants, so we're gonna do a bit of burning are we?
  Hands up all those who know how to start a fire!

They all look at each other and think for a while

All Daaaa!
Wimpy How do you make a fire then?

Music No 3

Uptempo number sung by ranchers

The Narrators stand up as all the other characters put their heads down into a still life position

Narrator 1 Poor Do Do, she was only trying to warn them about the
  Ranchers.
Narrator 2 Who are going to burn down the Forest to make Burgers.
Narrator 3 *(addressing the audience)* How many of YOU eat Burgers?
Narrator 4 Dead Animal!
Narrator 5 Dead Forests!
Narrator 6 If only she could make them listen!

Music No 4

An instrumental piece for a Butterfly Dance, watched by all the Animals in the Forest

Music No 5

Vulture Music begins - A skulking tune

The Vultures shuffle around the acting area, looking as nasty and sly as possible. They seem extremely pleased with themselves and every now and then break out into cackles of laughter. The Animals are watching them cautiously. They chuckle to themselves after each line has been delivered

Vulture 1 There's gonna be a lot of dead Animals around here soon!
Vulture 2 Frizzled Fried Frogs! Baked Bat! Medium Cooked Monkey!
Vulture 3 I like mine well done!
Vulture 1 Oh there's definitely gonna be a lot of dead Animals around here soon.

A rather unintelligent looking Vulture suddenly has a thought

Vulture 4 Is that 'cos the Ranchers are gonna burn down the Forest?

All the Vultures hold their heads in despair as the Animals hear what he has said. They all look at him

Oops!

The Animals start to whisper and a sense of panic becomes evident. The whispered message goes around each group of Animals like 'Chinese Whispers'

Animals Did you hear that. The Ranchers are going to burn down the Forest... etc etc

Music No 6

A full Chorus number linked to the theme of 'Fire'

The Do Do enters

Do Do I did try to tell you what was going to happen but you wouldn't listen to me, would you? Why do you think there is only one of me left?
Bee Because you bored the other Do Dos to death!
Baboon Listen Do Do, we've got more important things to worry about than how many of you there are left!
Monkey Yeah, like what's for dinner!
Leopard You're always thinking about food.

Do Do You just don't understand do you? You are all going to become chips very shortly!

Baboon And you're going to become stuffed if you don't shut up!

Bee And don't call me shortly!

Monkey I like chips!

Leopard There he goes again!

Monkey I'll have you know, I've got the appetite of an Ox.

Leopard Yeah, you've also got his brains!

Monkey Excuse me for breathing!

Do Do Look you're gonna need some help...

Bee Ha! A Do Do with a sense of humour... Shove off you boring ball of fluff.

The Do Do turns and exits

Parrot As if we need help... *(looks around)* We need help!

Beetles *(singing)* Help! We need somebody... Ooo!

Butterfly What about Noah Junior? He'll help.

Beetles *(singing)* Help! Not just anybody... Oooo!

Parrot Nora Junior? Never heard of him.

Leopard It's Noah, you baboon!

The Baboons stand up

Oops! Sorry! Just Monkeying around! Ha!

Butterfly Noah Junior is the one whose Great, Great, Grandad built the Ark which helped the Animals escape from the flood.

Elephant They said to build the Ark it took a Hard Day's Night.

All the Animals look and point at the Beetles

All Don't!

Parrot So let's go and find this Nora chap then!

All It's Noah!

Parrot Yeah alright! Keep your fur on!

Butterfly And besides, no one knows where he lives.

Monkey And I'm hungry!

Elephants We'll show you where he lives.

Music No 7

An instrumental piece as Animals all follow the Elephants off

Monkey *(left on his own)* But it's dinner time. We can't go now, it's dinner time. I can't walk on an empty stomach. Hello? Is anyone listening to me? *(exits after them)*

Narrator 1 So off the Animals went in search of Nora Junior.
All It's Noah!
Narrator 1 Sorry!
Narrator 2 In the hope that he would be able to solve their problems.
Narrator 3 Some hope!
Narrator 4 And as for their problems....

They all turn to face the Ranchers

Wimpy So how do you start a fire then?
Maurice You've got no brains have you?
Wimpy I might have!
Ken He just hasn't found them yet.
Mac Everyone knows you start a fire by rubbing two things together.
Pete Ahhh! Like what?
King Ears!
Ken No! Rubbing two heads together should do it!
Mac I'll rub your two heads together in a minute... Now think!
King Nothing's happening!
Maurice Think Stones.
King There's still nothing happening.
Sam Big Stones or little Stones?
Ken Rolling Stones! *(proceeds to give a Mick Jagger impersonation)*
Maurice Okay idiots. Think Wood.
Pete What Wood?
Ken No! It's 'Who Would?'
Mac Who Would What?
Pete What?
Ken Exactly!
Wimpy So how do you start a fire then?
Maurice Oh I give in!

*The Scene changes and we now see a group of Bats in a Bat Cave watching
Noah, a strange Professor type character, scribbling equations onto a board.
The Bats are rather squashed together and talk with Birmingham accents*

Kevin I'm Kevin, the Tropical Fruit Bat!
Kelvin I'm Kelvin, the Citrus Fruit Bat!
Keith I'm Keith, the Opel Fruit Bat!
Kenneth I'm Kenneth, the SQUASHED Fruit Bat!
Kelvin That's only 'cos...
All We want to be together!

Noah suddenly starts to panic

Noah Oo... I... um... er... um... oh!

Keith What's the matter with him then?
Kevin I dunno!

Noah is now searching around on his knees

Noah Well they were... um... er... well... sort of... Ahh!
Keith He's lost his marbles!
Kevin He's a sandwich short of a picnic!
Kelvin I think he's Bats!
Kenneth No! We're Bats!

Music No 8

Song to be sung by the Bats

Scene change to the Animals who have entered. The Vultures are also there, and are seen to be listening with great interest

Elephant Noah! We need your help.

All the Animals look at the Beetles again

All Don't!
Monkey And I need some food.
Noah Ah... Well... it's... um... just that... I... er... oh!
Leopard Noah! The Ranchers are going to burn down the Forest and we need you to help us.
Noah I can't make any decisions without my glasses.

All the Animals look at the audience in despair

Baboon Er Noah? Have you tried looking on your head?
Noah Now don't get clever with me, sonny. How can I look on my head when I haven't got my glasses to see with?
Bee Do you seriously think that this idiot is going to be able to help us? *(to Noah)* They're on your head you daft sprout!
Noah Now that is quite remarkable. I don't recall putting them there. Mmmm... Much better. Now then. How can I help you?
Leopard We need you to build us an Ark, so as we can escape from the Ranchers and their fires.
Parrott And we need it A.S.A.P.
Noah A.S.A.P.?
All As stupid as Parrots!

Feathers fly everywhere to show the Parrots disgust

Noah An Ark you say! Fascinating! So how do you make an Ark thing then?
Kevin Well, you're gonna need some Jewson Bricks!
Kelvin Some Jewson Tiles!
Keith Jewson Nails!
Kenneth Jewson Timber!
Kevin *(shouts)* TIMBER!

Everyone ducks and Kevin shrugs

Kelvin Jewson Sand!
Kenneth Jewson Cement!
Monkey And some Jewson Biscuits!

Everyone groans

Parrot We'll leave it to you Nora.
All It's Noah!

Animals exit and we see that the Vultures are still there

Noah I'll be fine... just as long as I can find a book with an Ark in it... Oh dear, I can't remember where I put my books... What am I going to do?

Music No 9

Vultures Music as they enter

Vulture I Here you are Noah. *(gives Noah a large 'Ark' book)*
Noah Oh thank you vultures, that's very kind of you.
Vulture 2 Our pleasure, Noah!

They snigger and exit

Noah A book on how to build an Ark. I hope you're going to help me Bats!
Kelvin *(struggling)* Ah... well we would Noah, but er...
All We want to be together!
Kenneth And besides, it's Kevin's Birthday today.
Kevin Is it?
Keith Happy Birthday Kevin.
Kelvin Yeah, Happy Birthday, Mate.
Kevin Oh Great! It's my Birthday and I didn't even know!
Noah Yes Alright. Alright. I get the message. I'll just have to build this Ark on my own then.
Kevin Did you get me any presents?
Noah Right... Pencil? Check! Book? Check! Glasses? Phew! Check! *(exits)*

Kenneth It's not really your Birthday Kevin. We only said it was your Birthday to get off helping Noah build the Ark.
Kelvin Yeah, We don't want to build Arks.
Keith We want to hang around.
Kenneth Doing nothing.
Kevin Didn't you even make me a cake?

The Bats exit leaving Kevin on his own

(singing)   Happy Birthday To Me.
                               Happy Birthday To Me.
                               Happy Birthday Dear Kevin.

One of the other Bats enters back on and drags him off. Kevin finishes the song in a hurry

                         Happy Birthday To Me!

Noah is seen in a different area looking for ingredients according to the book

Noah Mmm, according to this book, I need a tongue of gooseberry, the hair of the dog, a fist of fur, bark off a bending tree, extra large stinging nettles, and several cups of Iguana spit! It all sounds very odd to me but, oh well, we'll put it all together and see what happens! *(exits)*
Narrator 5 So the Animals left Noah the responsibility of making an ark to help them escape from the Ranchers and their fires.
Narrator 2 And off into the Forest he went looking for the rather strange ingredients.
Narrator 6 What a fool! He had been tricked!
Narrator 4 SOMEONE had changed the wording in Noah's book.
Narrator 3 He was looking for things that weren't going to help him at all!
Narrator 1 SOMEONE knew that by sending him off on a wild goose chase, it would enable the Ranchers to start their fires and burn down the rainforest.

They all look towards the Vultures, who sit chuckling to themselves

Music No 10

Vulture Music begins as they start talking

Vulture 1 He fell for it and now the Animals will never escape.
Vulture 2 A very good idea of yours.
Vulture 1 Why thank you!
Vulture 2 No! Thank YOU!

Vulture 1 No! Thank you!

They all join in thanking each other

Vulture 2 ...as if those things would make an Ark! Ha!
Vulture 3 Let's tell the Ranchers what we've done.
All *(excitedly)* Yes... Let's... Let's!
Vulture 1 They'll be very pleased with us.
Vulture 2 VERY pleased!
Vulture 3 They'll be able to make their Burgers now!
Vulture 4 Errr! Is that 'cos... the Ranchers are gonna burn down the Forest?

They all hold their heads in despair again

Music No 11

Song sung by the Vultures thinking they have done a good deed

The Animals enter

Butterfly We'll never escape from the Ranchers now.
Panda He didn't even know what an Ark was!
Monkey Our homes are going to be destroyed.
Baboon And we're going to become Burgers!
Parrot I thought he was quite a nice Nora.

They all sigh

Leopard Isn't there anything we can do?

They all put their heads down as if sad

The Do Do enters

Music No 12

A slow song for the Do Do to sing

Baboon Oh you're not still here you flaffing, feathered, fruit cake?
Leopard What are you gonna winge about this time?
Parrot I suppose you're going to tell us that we'll never be able to escape from the Ranchers.
Butterfly And that Noah doesn't know how to build an Ark.

The Do Do tries to speak

Bee Don't deny it. You just wanna get your own back on us because you think you know it all!

The Do Do tries to speak again

Don't interupt me when I'm in full flow. It's not often it happens. Next you'll be telling us that Noah has been tricked.
Do Do He has!
Bee See, there you go again, interrupting me every time I... *(pause)* What do you mean, 'He has?'
Do Do Noah has been tricked by those Vultures. That's what I've been trying to tell you. They took his, 'How To Build An Ark Book' and changed all the words to confuse him. He's now in the Rainforest looking for totally the wrong materials. We need to do something, and fast!
Monkey Yeah, like having somethmg to eat.
Elephant So what do you suggest then, Do Do?
Do Do Well, it may not be much, but I think I've got a plan.

They all crowd together to listen

The scene changes to the Ranchers

King Rubbing two noses together might do it!
Mac You're such a bright spark aren't you?
Pete *(laughing)* Ha! Bright spark... Fire... get it?
Maurice I am losing my patience with you lot. How long is it going to take you to work out how to start a fire?
Ken About this long. *(chuckles to himself as he indicates a length with his hands)*
Sam I don't see why we can't just use matches! *(takes a box of matches from his pocket)*

They all look angrily at him

Maurice Oh Great! So we have wasted 2 hours 47 minutes trying to work out how to start a fire, when Mr. Brain Cell over there kindly decides to produce a box of matches!
Wimpy So how do you start a fire then?

They all sigh

Music No 13

Vultures Music starts as Vultures enter

Vulture 2 Hello Ranchers.

The Ranchers suddenly try and look tough again

Mac   Don't waste our time Vultures, 'cos we are...
All   The Ranchers. *(motif)*
Vulture 3   On the contrary Ranchers.
Vulture 1   We are here with some extremely good news.
Vulture 3   Cunning news!
Vulture 2   Vital news!
Narrator 5   So the Vultures explained how they had tricked Noah.
Narrator 3   Leaving the Animals and the Forest totally vulnerable.
Narrator 1   Ready to be burnt!
Narrator 2   They began discussing how they would teach the Animals a lesson.
Narrator 4   They began drawing up plans!
Narrator 6   But the Animals had plans of their own!

Scene changes back to Animals

Do Do   Humans are afraid of disease, right?
Elephants   Right!
Do Do   And they wont go near anything that has a disease, right?
Butterflies   Right!
Monkey   And it's nearly time for something to eat, right?
All   Wrong!
Do Do   So if we make out that one of us has a disease and it's spreading through the Forest.
Baboon   Like Wild Fire...

They all look at him

  Oops, sore point, sorry!
Do Do   Then they wont come anywhere near us.
Parrot   In fact they'll probably disappear as quick as... *(tries to click his fingers, but can't)* Oh well!
Leopard   So which of us is going to have this disease then?
Bee   Well there's only one Animal that's stupid enough and ugly enough to look like he's got a disease!
Do Do   Oh! And who's that?
All   The Lesser Spotted, Half Witted, Oriental, Fire Bellied Toad!

They all turn to look at him and he's picking his nose

Toad   What have I done?
Do Do   Perfect!

Music No 14

Vulture Music as the Vultures enter

Vulture 1 What do you mean there's a disease in the Forest?
Vulture 3 Oh No!
Vulture 2 We heard the Animals talking about it.
Vulture 3 Oh, no!
Vulture 1 And how did this disease find it's way into the Forest?
Vulture 2 Apparently, the Lesser Spotted, Half Witted, Oriental, Fire Bellied Toad brought it in!
Vulture 3 Oh...

They cover his beak before he says anymore

Vulture 1 The Ranchers aren't going to like this one bit!
Vulture 4 Is that 'cos... The Ranchers ... *(thinks)*... No!
Mac What do you mean there's a disease in the Forest, it wasn't there yesterday!
Ken Do you want us to go and sort it out Big Mac?
Pete Yeah! We'll go and get it!
Maurice You will get it if you go anywhere near it, you prunes!
All Yeah good point. Why didn't you think of that you prune? etc etc
Maurice You do know what a disease is don't you?
All Course we do... *(pause)*... What is it Wimpy?
Wimpy *(sticks his thumb up)* Don't you just love being in control!
Mac Right, send the Vultures back into the Forest. Tell them to check and see if Noah has got this disease.
King That's a bit selfish of him if he's got the disease all to himself.
Sam My Mum always told me to share what I had with others.
Maurice Thank goodness you didn't share out your one Brain Cell, boy, would you have been in trouble then!
Mac It could be, that this disease doesn't affect humans, only Animals. BUT - if the Vultures come back and say that Noah has got the disease... We're out of here.

He points across the face of the Rancher to his side and all the others repeat the phrase and copy him. The Rancher at the end of the line gets a finger up his nose

Ken Can't we just hang around for a bit... I've never seen a disease before.
Narrator 1 So off the Vultures went deep into the Forest to find Noah.
Narrator 2 Who was still trying to collect various materials to help him build an Ark.

Narrator 3 The Vultures knew the hot, steamy Rainforest well, but they felt uneasy.

Narrator 4 And as they cautiously approached the spot where Noah was.

Narrator 5 The canopy of water soaked leaves seemed to whisper and laugh.

Narrator 6 As if it knew what was going to happen.

Noah Right! I think that just about does it. *(suddenly turns round and reveals his rather spotty face)*

The Vultures scream and run off. They think Noah has the disease

Funny! I thought I heard something. Perhaps it was the tongue of a Gooseberry giving a yelp! Or maybe the lip of a flower having a moan... Or the mouth of a cave giving a shout... Ha! How marvellous! *(exits)*

Scene change back to Ranchers with the Vultures having just arrived

Vulture 3 Oh Ranchers! A slight bit of bad news I'm afraid!

Vulture 2 However, we don't want you to get too upset!

Vulture 1 It's just that...

Mac Get on with it!

Pete Otherwise you'll find out which falls faster; a feather or a Vulture!

Vulture 2 Well we found Noah.

Vulture 3 On his own in the Forest.

Vulture 1 And he's got the disease!!

Vulture 2 H..orrible spots all over his face!

Vulture 1 H..uge!

Vulture 3 H..umungous!

Vulture 2 H..orrendous!

Vulture 1 H..ideous!

Vulture 4 H..enry Kelly!

All Henry Kelly?

Vulture 4 It's the only thing I could think of beginning with the letter 'H'.

Mac That's it then. We can't burn down the Forest if there's a disease about. We'd die before we even lit the match!

Wimpy So that's how you start a fire!

Vulture 2 When you say 'die', you mean this disease will kill you?

Sam Yes you great big feathered Duvet, course it will kill you!

Vultures *(scared)* We're coming with you then.

King So what now, Mac?

Pete Yeah, so what other destructive things can we do?

Ken We could flood the Sahara.

Maurice We could straighten the Leaning Tower of Pisa.

Mac We could find some more Forests.

King Yeah! Let's go and find some more Forests.

Ken And burn them down!

Wimpy It's not as though anyone really needs them!
Pete But we need them!
Maurice For Burgers!
Mac 'Cos we are... *(motif)*
All The Ranchers.
Mac Big Mac.
Ken Ken Tucky.
Pete Pete Zerut.
Maurice Maurice the Little Chef.
Sam Uncle Sam.
Wimpy Wimpy.
King Burger King.
All You Got It!
Mac Let's Go!

They exit with 'macho' walks, verbally abusing the audience

Vultures 'Cos we are... *(they try the Motif but get it wrong)*... forget it!

They exit in the same way

Scene changes back to Animals

Parrot Do you think the plan has worked, Do Do?
Leopard Do you think the Ranchers have gone?
Monkey And taken the Vultures with them, I hope!
Elephant Noah's coming and... and he's got the disease!
Do Do But he can't have the disease you silly Animals... It was made up!
Noah Yoo Hoo! It's Me!

The Animals hide

I say this is no time to play games. I have some incredible news!
Do Do Er Noah, I don't want to worry you, but you've got the most horrific
spots all over your face!
Noah Correct! And you would like to know how I came to get these little
fellas. Well, I suffer from Tropical Hay Fever... Same time every year...
Out they pop. Colourful little bumps aren't they?
Bee I suffer from Tropical Hay Fever as well... It's the Pollen.
Baboon But you're a Bee!
Bee I know! Strange innit?

They all look at the audience with raised eyebrows

Noah But the best bit of news, is that I saw the Ranchers AND the
Vultures running out of the Forest screaming about a disease!

Vulture 4 has been left behind and suddenly pops up

Vulture 4   Is that 'cos The Ranchers... No!

They push the Vulture away

Parrot   So the plan did work!
Monkey   Thanks, Do Do!
Bee   And Noah.
Baboon   I do have one question though Noah. What happened to all the ingredients you wrongly collected to help you build the Ark?
Noah   A good question little fella. It just so happened that after being tricked by the Vultures into collecting the wrong things, I was carefully carrying them back when I accidentally dropped them all over the Forest floor.
Parrot   Oh well, it wouldn't have made an Ark anyway!
Noah   Ah! But it did make something however... besides a mess! As soon as the ingredients touched the floor of the Forest, everything started to grow again... Instantly. Even the damaged plants and species were, given a new life!
Elephants   We've got some things to celebrate!
All   Party!

Music No 15

Song - Up-tempo Jungle Dance Number

The song should suddenly stop dead

Narrator 1   While you've been watching this performance, 3,600 acres of Rainforest has been destroyed.
Narrator 2   Cut to the ground, burnt to nothing!
Narrator 3   Gone Forever!
Narrator 4   Lost!
Narrator 5   There are no special formulas to make them grow again.
Narrator 6   And the children of tomorrow will never know it was there.
All Narrators   We must all become Keepers Of The Forest.

Music No 16

Song - Slow Chorus Number that promotes the message of hope sung by the entire cast

The End

THE
GARDEN PLOT

A Musical Play by Darren Vallier

When the House Owners decide to make some changes to the Garden, certain decisions need to be made. But, whatever you do... don't get bugged!

A Musical play which conveys the feelings of everyday garden animals and creatures. How will they react when the House Owners decide to make some drastic changes to the garden? The storyline holds many environmental issues and talking points but whatever you do... don't get bugged!

All the scenes take place in a garden.

First performed in February 1992 at Patcham Junior School

CHARACTERS

2	Gnomes
5	Bugs, including a Lead Bug and a Little Bug
5	Fairies, including a Lead Fairy
	Sunflowers, including a Little Sunflower
	Cats
	Vegetables

Plus a variety of other Chorus Animals

The script can easily be adapted to include any number of other cast members

Motif by all Bugs

BUG 1 Looking good.
BUG 2 Looking good.
BUG 3 Looking good.
BUG 4 Looking good.
LITTLE BUG Looking good.
BUG 1 We look for danger.
BUG 2 We look for fun.
BUG 3 We look for trouble.
BUG 4 We look for music.
LITTLE BUG All day and night we party. *(wiggly movements)*

Bug 4 looks at sleeping animals whilst Bug 1 admires someone in the audience (pouting, eyebrows etc)

BUG 4 Hey, Hugh!
OTHERS Yes?
BUG 4 No, not you... Hugh.
BUG 2 Who me?
BUG 3 No, he wants Hugh.
BUG 2 But I am me!
BUG 4 Yes you're you, but I want Hugh.

Confusion on the faces

BUG 3 But if he's Hugh and...
BUG 1 Oh shut up, can't you see I'm... working! Anyway, what do you want?
BUG 4 *(looking at sleeping animals)* How can we party now?

Other Bugs agree

BUG 1 We'll wake them up.

Other Bugs agree as if they're clever

BUG 4 I knew that!
BUG 1 Hit me!

The other Bugs do as they're told and hit him

BUG 1 Not me... the band!

Song No 2

Song, 'Bug Boogie'

As the Lead Bug sings, the other animals all scream as if he is a rock star

BUG 2 If you're going to keep showing off... I'm leaving!
BUG 3 Me too!
BUG 4 Me two and a half!

Bug Boogie is played whilst Bugs leave and a chicken struts across the stage behind the wall. The chicken looks at the audience and then struts off

Two gnomes can be seen sitting slightly apart from each other on toadstools or mushrooms. One of the Gnomes is fishing, the other one is listening to a Walkman and wobbling about

GNOME 1 You know, we have sat here in this garden for twelve years. *(holds up 7 fingers)* We eat, drink, breathe, burp and still no one takes a blind bit of notice of us, do they?

There is a long pause as this particular Gnome cannot believe his eyes. For the other Gnome is jigging about and singing rather loudly and poorly

A chicken passes across the back, looks at the audience and Gnomes and decides to stay and watch. (Constant smile of amusement on the chicken's face)

GNOME 1 Oi... cloth ears... wrinkly... nit wit... pea brain... UGLY!

The chicken is now rolling about as the Gnome picks up a flower pot and throws it at the second Gnome. The chicken's legs wiggle in the air

GNOME 2 What was that for?
GNOME 1 I was talking to you and you weren't listening.
GNOME 2 I'm hungry!
GNOME 1 See, you're still not listening to me now.

Gnome 1 slides off his toadstool and goes over to hit Gnome 2

GNOME 1 Look.

GNOME 2 Don't you touch me!
GNOME 1 If you're hungry then go and get some chicken.

The chicken looks a little concerned but then smiles, points and calls to his chicken friends

Enter more chickens

GNOME 2 Oh and where am I going to find a chicken around here, Big Nose?

Gnome 2 looks pretty pleased with himself and folds his arms in triumph

GNOME 1 Big nose? Big nose? Listen smarty-pants, I'll have you know that if it wasn't for you I'd probably have been promoted to a Metro-Gnome by now.
GNOME 2 Okay, okay keep your beard on!
GNOME 1 I remember when there were six Gnomes here to keep those cats away.
GNOME 2 What happened to them then?
GNOME 1 Well... one got cat-napped, one fell in the pond and drowned, one was made Gnomeless, and three were got rid of with the National Elf Service.

Gnome 2 counts on his fingers (so do the Chickens)

I mean what would you do if a cat came along right now?
GNOME 2 Well... I would... *(pauses and thinks, then produces from somewhere a huge 'Gnome Handbook' and flicks through it)* Chase it off!
GNOME 1 You couldn't chase off a <u>stuffed</u> chicken.

Chickens make flustered noises, and now look in interest, and look a little bit angry

GNOME 2 Yes I could. I'll show you. I bet I could scare them off. *(points to a section of the audience)*
GNOME 1 What them? No you couldn't.
GNOME 2 Yes I could. You watch! *(gets off his toadstool turns round and begins a big build up getting himself ready. Then he turns round and says, 'Boo' in a pathetic voice)*

The chickens laugh

GNOME 1 Hopeless! Look this is how you scare them off. I'll scare that lot over there. *(points to another part of the audience)*

An even bigger build up occurs this time but with an even more pathetic, 'Boo' at the end of it

A chicken by this time has started to make his way towards the two Gnomes who are laughing and arguing with each other. The chicken produces a huge squawk which frightens the Gnomes half to death. Gnome 1 jumps up into Gnome 2's arms

GNOME 1 *(shaking and stuttering with other Gnome's head moving up and down on stutter)* Give me a hanky.

Gnome 2 gives him one. Gnome 1 blows his nose on it, and puts it into his pocket, feeling the wetness

GNOME 2 You know what...
GNOME 1 We're just hopeless being Gnomes!
GNOME 2 And I'm still hungry!

They sit back on their toadstools

Song No 3

Song, 'Where's My Dinner'

It begins to rain. The chickens run off

The Gnomes moan and tut, and then put umbrellas up and leave kicking and slashing, and the sunflowers make their way around the wall to the front for dance. That is except for the Little Sunflower, who, throughout the dance tries to get over the wall, but is too small

Music No 4

Instrumental, 'Rain Ballet'. Sunflowers exit. The Little Sunflower finally gets to the top of the wall and produces a big smile, which soon disappears when he realises that the dance has finished and everyone has gone

Song No 5

Song, 'As All The Seasons Change'

Sunflowers appear again and take the Little Sunflower off, the Gnomes make their way back to their places on their toadstools

GNOME 1 You know we have sat here in this garden for twelve...
GNOME 2 We've done this bit.
GNOME 1 What?
GNOME 2 We've done this bit.
GNOME 1 Have we? Oh right. Then where are we? Ah, that means you should be crying.
GNOME 2 Oh right! *(cries really loudly)* How's that?
GNOME 1 Yes that's... er... very good, but perhaps a little over the top.
GNOME 2 Oh right... *(cries a little quieter)* Oh, I do hate weepies, they always make me cry.

Gnome 1 produces the hanky, looks at it, smiles and then hands it to Gnome 2

Thank you... Oh it does make me want to... Errrr! *(looks at hanky)*
GNOME 1 It makes you want to... Errrr! What's an Errrr?

As Gnome 2 makes the next speech, Gnome 1 hears noises and turns to see what it is

The Vegetables make their way on casually, finding a place to sit

Gnome 1 rubs his eyes and is not sure what he has seen. He thinks he's seeing things so dismisses it

GNOME 2 You've given me that hanky back, you've given me that soggy hanky!
GNOME 1 I'm going to swap you for a vegetable, *(turns away)* although there's not a great deal of difference.
GNOME 2 I heard that! Don't you ever, ever compare me to one of them. *(points to a Vegetable head right next to him, looks at audience, looks back at Vegetable)*

Both Gnomes then scream and run all over the place bumping into each other to 'Chase music'

The Vegetables hide themselves in a huddle as the Gnomes creep carefully back on, backwards. Therefore, they end up bumping into each other and hitting each other again

GNOME 2 You stupid...

GNOME 1 The... the... Vegetables they... were... here.

GNOME 2 *(smiles smugly)* You weren't scared were you?

GNOME 1 Me! Course not!

GNOME 2 Yes you were.

GNOME 1 No I wasn't.

GNOME 2 Yes you were. You weren't frightened of a Turnip were you?

GNOME 1 *(laughing)* No! I was scared of the Tomato!

GNOME 2 I want to be a Tomato!

GNOME 1 You've got the IQ of a Tomato. I want to be a Carrot!

GNOME 2 I want a leek! *(falls off toadstool laughing)*

GNOME 1 What's an IQ?

GNOME 2 I want to beat the living daylights out of that horrible, snivelling, muddy, little twerp of a cabbage.

GNOME 1 Oh you like him then!

Gnomes continue to laugh and take the mickey while the Vegetables look on not too impressed. Then suddenly there is an Adult voice over, plus the noise of footsteps as if two people are walking in the garden

GNOMES Sshhh... It's the house owners. The Big People!

ADULT VOICE The Gnomes must go, darling. They do make the garden look untidy. I think we should plant the Vegetables down there, make it their home. We'll throw the Gnomes on the tip!

Horrible Chord

There is now horror on the Gnomes' faces as the Vegetables disappear ready to bring on their furniture and bits

GNOME 1 Throw us away! They... they are joking! After all these years, they've now decided to throw us on a rubbish tip, and allow the Vegetables to make this their home, after all we've done, looking after this garden, clearing up the mess, making sure the cats don't come around.

Cats faces suddenly appear and 'Cat Music' is played

GNOME 2 Hey, hey calm down, we're not going to be thrown on any rubbish tip. *(pause)* We're gonna go somewhere where we'll be appreciated, looked after, treated like royalty - you know red carpet, royal waves, proper tea. *(mimes these actions while he is talking)*

GNOME 1 You mean we're gonna move on.

GNOME 2 That's precisely what I mean. We're gonna move on, just the two of us!

GNOME 1 But what about tidying up and... and the Animals, who will look after them when we've gone? We've got to say goodbye!

GNOME 2 Huh! They don't even know we exist.

Song No 6

Song, 'Movie Scene'

While this last speech and song takes place the Vegetables bring on the furniture and make themselves at home, including asking the Gnomes to move so as they can place things down. The Gnomes have one final look at the garden and then leave. The Vegetables wave

VEGETABLE 8 Oi, Fred. Turn the telly on will you. I don't wanna miss the adverts.

End of Act One

Interval

Act Two

Enter Animals talking, singing, dancing etc., The cats keep appearing and smiling, then disappearing (Cat Music played as animals look around)

ANIMAL 1 'Ere, shut up... shut up... something's not right.
ANIMAL 5 Well there's you for a start.
ANIMAL 7 You've never been right.

All the Animals look around and at each other, up and down, to try and discover what is not right

ANIMAL 10 I know, its the grass... it's been cut!
ANIMAL 1 No, that's not it.
ANIMAL 2 I got it, I got it... the sun's shining.

Others laugh. Animal 1 shakes his head

ANIMAL 4 I know, the flowers have grown.
ANIMAL 1 *(slightly angry)* No!
ANIMAL 6 Your nose has grown?
ANIMAL 1 NO!
ANIMAL 9 It's the smell!

All smell each other

ANIMAL 8 It's Daffy's perm!

Daffy feels her hair

ANIMAL 11 Benny's feet.
ANIMAL 3 Rodney's breath.
ANIMAL 6 I haven't got a perm!
SUNFLOWER 1 Jenny's glasses.
SUNFLOWER 2 Where are my glasses? *(panic while she looks for them)*

Some of the others try them on and then pass them on

ANIMAL 10 It's the Litter!

OTHERS   What litter?

The Band then throw litter on. All look at Animal 1 to see if that was it

ANIMAL 1   *(shouting)* No, it's not the litter.
ANIMAL 5   It's the birds' doo doos! *(smiling)*

All look at him, so he shrugs his shoulders and says

Sorry!
ANIMAL 1   He's right!
ANIMAL 5   What, it is the bird doo doos?
ANIMAL 1   No it's the Gnomes.
ANIMAL 10   It's the Gnomes' doo doos?
ANIMAL 1   No, it's the Gnomes... They've gone.

The Cats appear in various places about the garden, perhaps playing cards or holding knife and fork

And they've gone because of them. *(points up above)*

The Animals look confused and unsure

The House Owners.
OTHERS   Oh yeah right!
ANIMAL 1   And we didn't take a blind bit of notice of them, did we?
ANIMAL 2   We never talked to them!
ANIMAL 3   We never thanked them for clearing the garden.
ANIMAL 10   We didn't even know they were there!
ANIMAL 11   And I forgot to invite them to my birthday party!

The others pause, then look at him and say, 'Shut up!'

ANIMAL 1   And you know what that means, now that they've gone, don't you?

They all nod, and then shake their heads sheepishly

It means the Cats will now be around.

Vegetables begin to sneak off

ANIMAL 5 They are sure to have heard the news.

ANIMAL 2 And they're gonna think the garden is theirs!

ANIMAL 3 So what are we going to do?

ANIMAL 1 Shut up, I'm thinking.

The Lead Animal leaves mumbling to himself, followed by the others shrugging and not knowing what he's going to do

Music No 7

Instrumental, 'Cat Strut'

Animals enter, so the Cats run and hide, but keep popping heads out, licking paws, looking evil and listening. Occasionally they walk across the back carrying one of the Vegetables

ANIMAL 1 I've got it! *(starts looking through the Yellow Pages)*

ANIMAL 2 What's he got?

ANIMAL 3 Bad breath?

ANIMAL 4 False teeth?

ANIMAL 5 Nappy rash?

ANIMAL 6 A bald patch?

Animal 1 hasn't been listening and so continues

ANIMAL 1 We'll call the... *(whispers something)*

ANIMAL 11 The Fairies! *(hand over mouth and gets hit on the head)*

ANIMAL 10 Sshhh... don't mention the F word!

ANIMAL 4 What F word?

ANIMAL 6 Fairies! *(gets hit round the head)*

ANIMAL 3 Call them something else.

ANIMAL 7 Alright, how about Doughnuts?

ANIMAL 9 Or Cheesecake?

ANIMAL 11 What Cheesecake?

ANIMAL 2 There is no Cheesecake!

ANIMAL 5 We're just saying it instead of Fairies! *(gets hit around head)*

ANIMAL 8 What?

OTHERS Don't mention the Fairies!

All start hitting each other

ANIMAL 6 I don't see why we can't mention them!

ANIMAL 1 Because... Fairies are a last resort. They're not your normal type of fairy. They're not very intelligent, they're certainly not very helpful. I mean all they ever do is bop. *(sigh)* But it's all we've got left. Come on we had better go and find them.

Exit Animals

Enter Fairies with Lead Fairy bopping to rock music whilst the others stand watching in disbelief. (Boys could play Fairies - wearing ballet desses and wellington boots)

Lead Fairy suddenly stubs his toe and stops out of breath. Growls at audience. Other Fairies step forward

FAIRY 2 You look a bit tired!

LEAD FAIRY I'm alright!

FAIRY 3 Maybe it's time you became a normal Fairy!

FAIRY 4 You know, knock it on the head, stop bopping!

LEAD FAIRY Stop bopping! Stop bopping. You might as well ask me to stop breathing!

OTHER FAIRIES Oh no boss... we didn't mean... Boss we only thought...

LEAD FAIRY I'll give you three good reasons why I'm never going to stop bopping. A, it keeps me looking slim. 2, I enjoy it. And, D, *(to the band)* after 4 lads.

The Band count in 2 and start playing

Song No 8

Song, 'Me'

Enter Animals looking at the Fairies and at each other while Fairies finish off the song

ANIMAL 2 Look at em... They're just a bunch of old fairies!

The Fairies' heads turn

LEAD FAIRY Don't you ever call us... old! *(finger up nose routine)* We're actually very tough.

OTHERS Yeah. *(get back etc)*

ANIMAL 1 Are you THE FAIRIES?

Fairies make noises and Lead Fairy pulls them back

LEAD FAIRY Who wants to know?
ANIMAL 1 Now, Fairies... We know you're intelligent.
ANIMAL 9 I thought you said they were...

Animal 1 puts hand over Animal 9's mouth and smiles. Fairies discuss it for a bit

LEAD FAIRY We are!
ANIMAL 1 And we know you are extremely helpful!
ANIMAL 9 But you said... (*hand over mouth*)

Animal 9 tries to say something by wiggling about and waving his hands about. Fairies discuss it again

LEAD FAIRY We are.
OTHER FAIRIES Are we?
ANIMAL 1 And we know you know all the answers to all the questions in the whole of the world!

Fairies discuss it quicker this time

How can we get the Gnomes back?

Fairies look dumb

LEAD FAIRY Ah, we know all the answers to all the questions in the world... except for that one! (*does a quick embarrassed 'Ha'*)

Other Fairies laugh and nudge each other, but when Lead Fairy turns round they stop. Animals look a bit disappointed and sad now

Oh look, leave it to us... go home, put your feet up and let us do the job that we are best at!

Lead Fairy pushes the Animals off gently and then turns back to the other Fairies...

LEAD FAIRY PANIC!

They do by jumping up and down and running round in circles screaming

FAIRY 2 Helping people, we can't even help ourselves get dressed in the mornings.

FAIRY 4 *(to Lead Fairy)* Exactly how many times have you helped someone before?

LEAD FAIRY holds up 6 fingers, and then quickly withdraws them again.

FAIRY 3 None! None! Oh that's just great!

FAIRY 1 Hang on, hang on... remember we are THE FAIRIES.

Big noise from the others

LEAD FAIRY So let's do it... come on.

BAND Okay, get it right this time... after four... One, two... *(music starts)*

Song No 9

Exit Fairies to reprise of their song

Cat Music played throughout this next scene

Cats have entered and shown their faces again, but have had to hide because the Animals have resumed. The Cats get ready to pounce. The Animals look depressed and fed up. They sit and stand sighing and moving from one position to another. The Cats creep up behind them and pounce, but to no effect. The Cats look at each other and then at the Animals, in their hair, hands waved in front of the face, a silly dance etc... but nothing happens, so the cats sit down and join in the ritual sighing. (in line with each other and the Animals)

Suddenly voices are heard offstage. The Bugs enter

The Cats smile - food

BUG 1 Looking Good!

BUG 2 Looking Good!

BUG 3 Looking Good!

BUG 4 Looking Good!

The Bugs get into their line and Bug 1 counts them realising that Little Bug isn't there, and remembers what happened last time with the tricycle from the left. They prepare themselves... and in comes Little Bug on the tricycle from the right, and knocks them all down again. They struggle to their feet

BUG 3   Wow! I'd say this garden has gone to pot, ha! Gone to pot - get it?
BUG 2   Lovely!
BUG 1   Oh thank you. Didn't know you cared!
BUG 2   I don't!
BUG 1   Why not?
BUG 4   Oh this is too depressing for me, I'm off.
BUG 3   I wondered what the smell was! Ha, ha!

Bug 1 tells him to 'sshhh' and then goes after Bug 4

BUG 1   You mean to say you're gonna leave the party?
BUG 4   What party?

The Bugs start to sing the 'Bug Boogie' but realise that it isn't cheering the Animals up - so they stop

ANIMAL 1   Thanks for trying Bugs, but the Gnomes haven't returned and it's just not the same without them.
ANIMAL 7   We can't even scare the cats away.
ANIMAL 4   Only the Gnomes could do that.

The Bugs look at the Cats who wave and smile, do their nails etc.,

BUG 3   We need to cheer them up!
BUG 1   We need a plan!
LITTLE BUG   I have a plan!
BUG 2   We need a plan with a bit of sparkle!
LITTLE BUG   I have a plan with a bit of sparkle!
BUG 3   We need a plan with a bit of bite!
LITTLE BUG   *(angry now)* I have a plan with a bit of bite!
BUG 4   We need a whopper of a plan!
LITTLE BUG   I have a whopper of a plan!
BUG 1   We need a plan!

Little Bug grabs Bug 1 and pulls him down to his height

LITTLE BUG   I HAVE A PLAN!
BUG 1   Well why didn't you say so! *(tuts)*

The Bugs then get into a rugby scrum

LITTLE BUG A Cat wails best when you tread on its tail!

A Cat wails as a Bug treads on his tail

BUG 2 A Cat wails best when you kick it!

A Cat gets kicked and wails

BUG 3 No... a Cat wails best while standing on a wall!

Cat gets pushed off and wails

BUG 4 No... no... no... a Cat wails best when you put a bucket over its head.

A Cat wails from inside a bucket put there by a Bug

BUG 1 Hey... a Cat wails best if you give it some water. *(sprays water from a water pistol)*

During all this, the Bugs are holding certain still life positions when the suggestions are being made

Each time a wail occurs, the Band hold up result cards with marks out of ten on them. Other Cats hide, crouched down shaking

ADULT VOICE OVER Right that's it we're moving... There are too many Cats in this area, and I hate Cats! Horrible racket!

A big cheer goes up from all the Animals who then congratulate the Bugs and Cats (much to the Cats' amazement)

BUG 1 Of course that was my original plan! *(looking chuffed with himself)*
LITTLE BUG It was my plan.
BUG 1 Of course that was his original plan. *(said with same smile on face which soon disappears)*
ANIMAL 8 *(pointing)* Hey look... The Fairies have managed to find the Gnomes!
ANIMAL 6 And here they come now!

Fairies and Gnomes enter singing and dancing. Cheers from all the animals

ANIMAL 1 How did you talk them into coming back?
FAIRY 1 Well, we thought of all the good points the garden had like...
FAIRY 3 Damp, birds' doo doos and Vegetables.
FAIRY 1 And that didn't help one bit!
FAIRY 2 So we decided it was best if we threatened to show them what was under our skirts.
LEAD FAIRY So now there's only one thing for it... *(smiles)* BOPPING!
OTHERS Hooray!

Fairies look at each other as if to say, 'Oh No!'

The Vegetables are well on their way to leaving having seen the Gnomes return, but they themselves do take part in the Finale with full company

Song No 10

Finale Song, 'Funny Kind of Love' or 'Bug Boogie'

Followed by full company singing, 'Movie Scene'

The End

The Darren Vallier
Song Book

Containing **17 songs** from his shows;

The Garden Plot
The Ivory Forest

and many others, including 'A Ring of Roses'
soon to be a West End Musical (Autumn 1998)

ISBN 1 874009 67 8

and

'When Saturday Comes'

by
Darren Vallier

Two rival teenage gangs compete for the local
'park' territory, but how will they settle their dispute -
'When Saturday Comes'?

A play for school and youth production
complete with 10 original songs

ISBN 1 874009 37 6